If you like to color and you've been looking for something with a bit more life in the images than the books you find at the store then you will not be disappointed. This book is a collection of 12 hand drawn coloring pages and some of my favorite quotes; an adult coloring book with a personal flare.

Art has always been a part of my life. It is the language of my soul and I feel a complete sense of peace when I'm creating. My drawings are intuitive and inspired by the mhendi designs I studied in my childhood. For me the process is meditative. All of the images are drawn free hand with a ballpoint pen on paper, then scanned onto the computer.

I hope you enjoy coloring them as much as I enjoyed drawing them. May you life be filled with joy and gratitude.

Second edition
Follow us of facebook; Coloring with Friends

Before we get started I want to give a special thanks to all of my friends, family, and coworkers who've supported me, and encouraged me to share my work with the world.

Thank you to my parents for sending me to class and thank you to my teacher for giving me a language to express myself in.

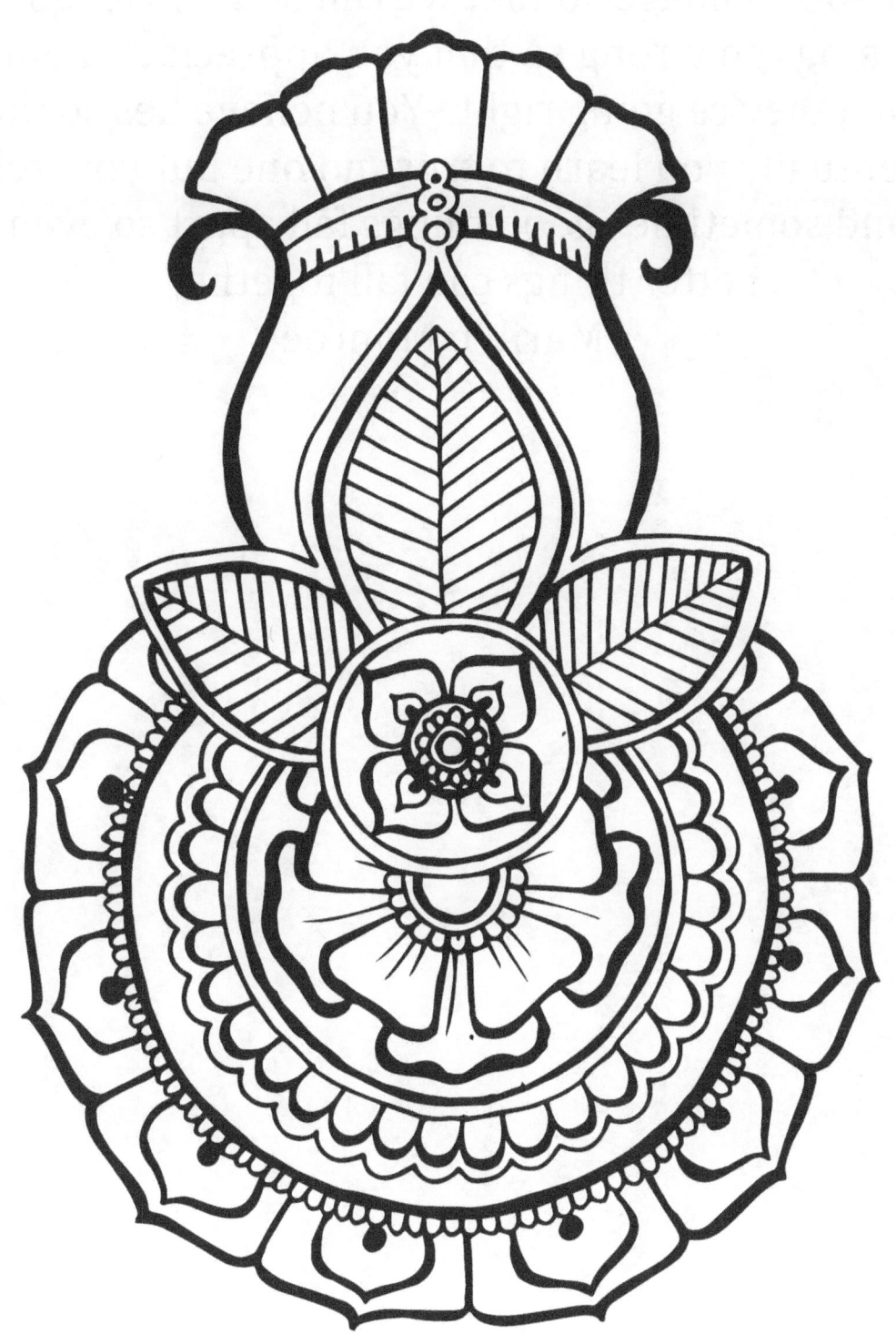

I believe that everything happens for a reason.
People change so that we can learn to let go.
Things go wrong so that you appreciate them
when they're going right. You believe lies so that
eventually you learn to trust no one but yourself,
and sometimes good things fall apart so even
better things can fall together.
~Marilyn Monroe

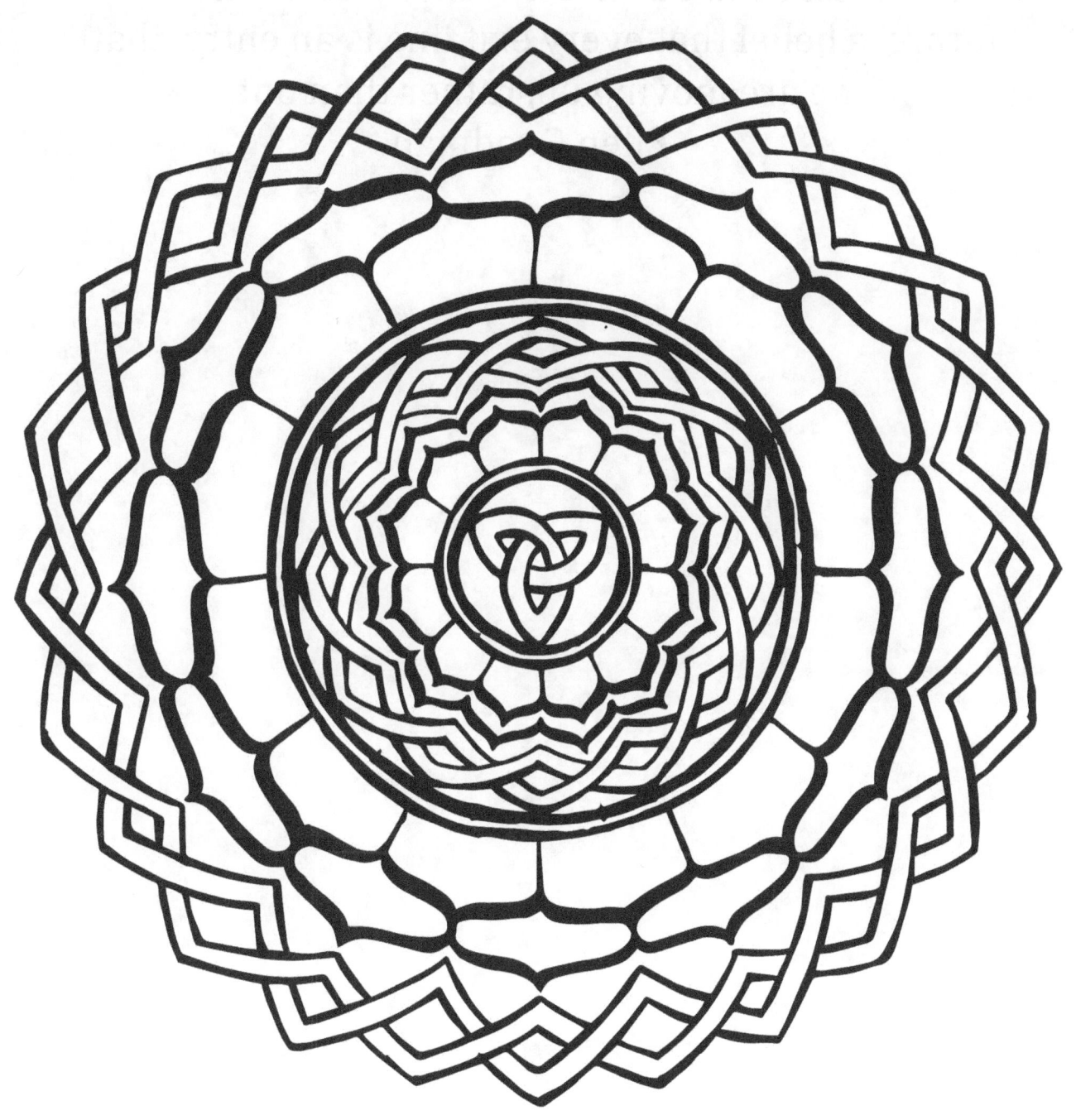

8 6/13

There's a trick to the "graceful exit." It begins with the vision to recognize when a job, a life stage, or a relationship is over-and let it go. It means leaving what's over without denying its validity or its past importance to our lives. It involves a sense of future, a belief that every exit line is an entry, that we are moving up, rather than out.

~Ellen Goodman

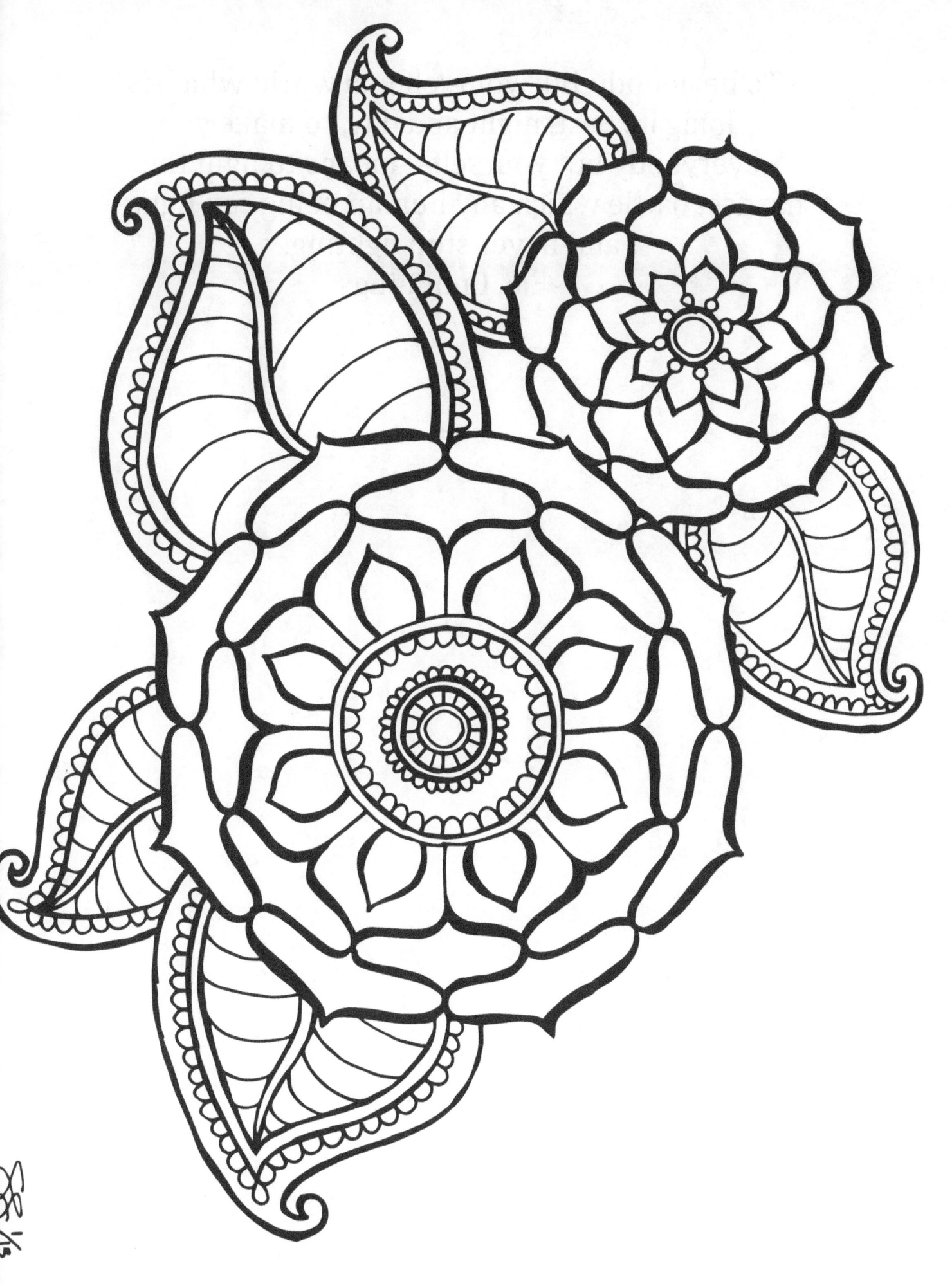

To be nobody-but-yourself in a world which is doing its best, night and day, to make you everybody but yourself—means to fight the hardest battle which any human being can fight—and never stop fighting.
~E.E. Cummings

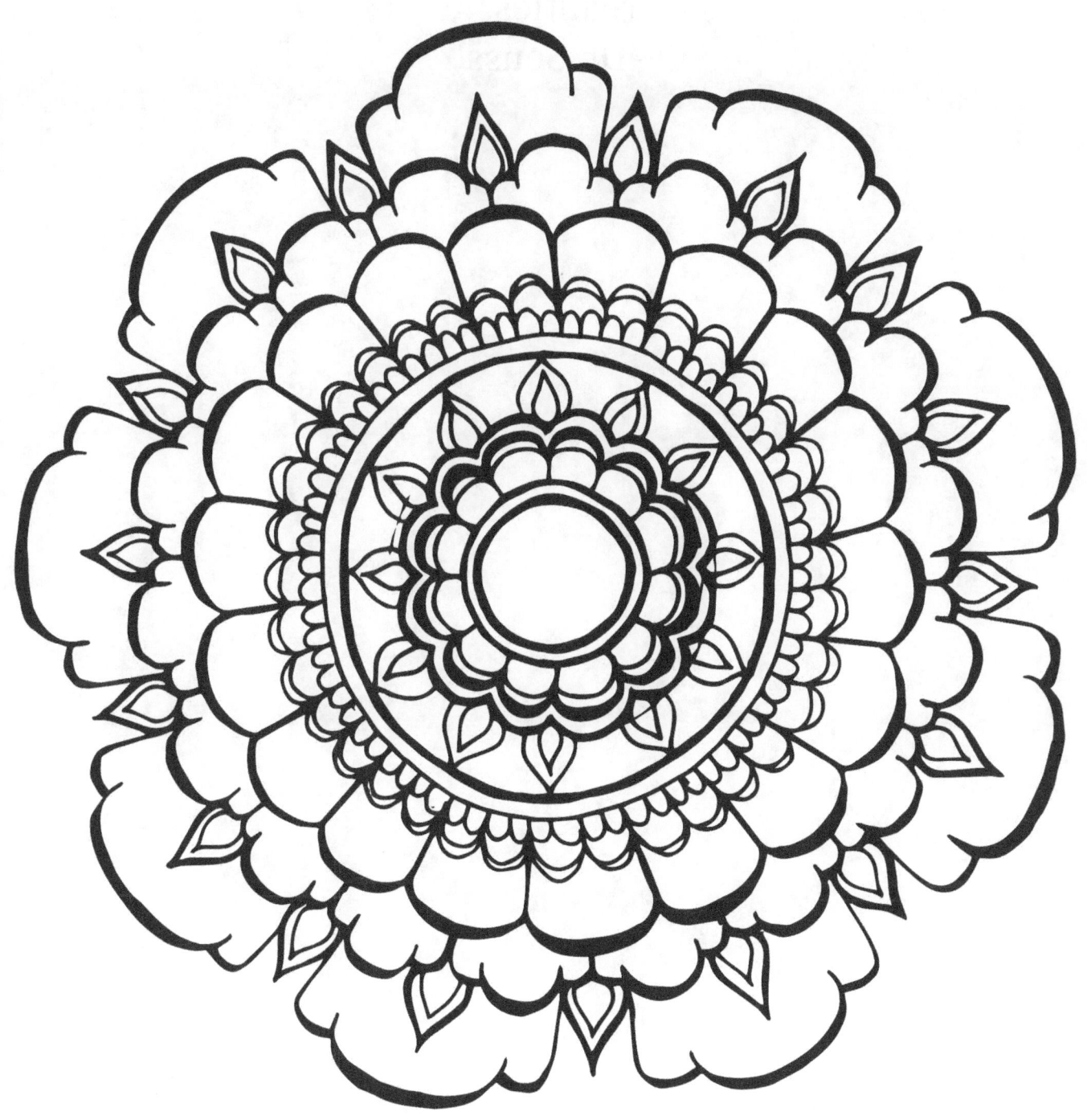

Fantasy is a necessary ingredient in living, it's a way of looking at life through the wrong end of a telescope, and that enables you to laugh at life's realities.
~Dr. Seuss

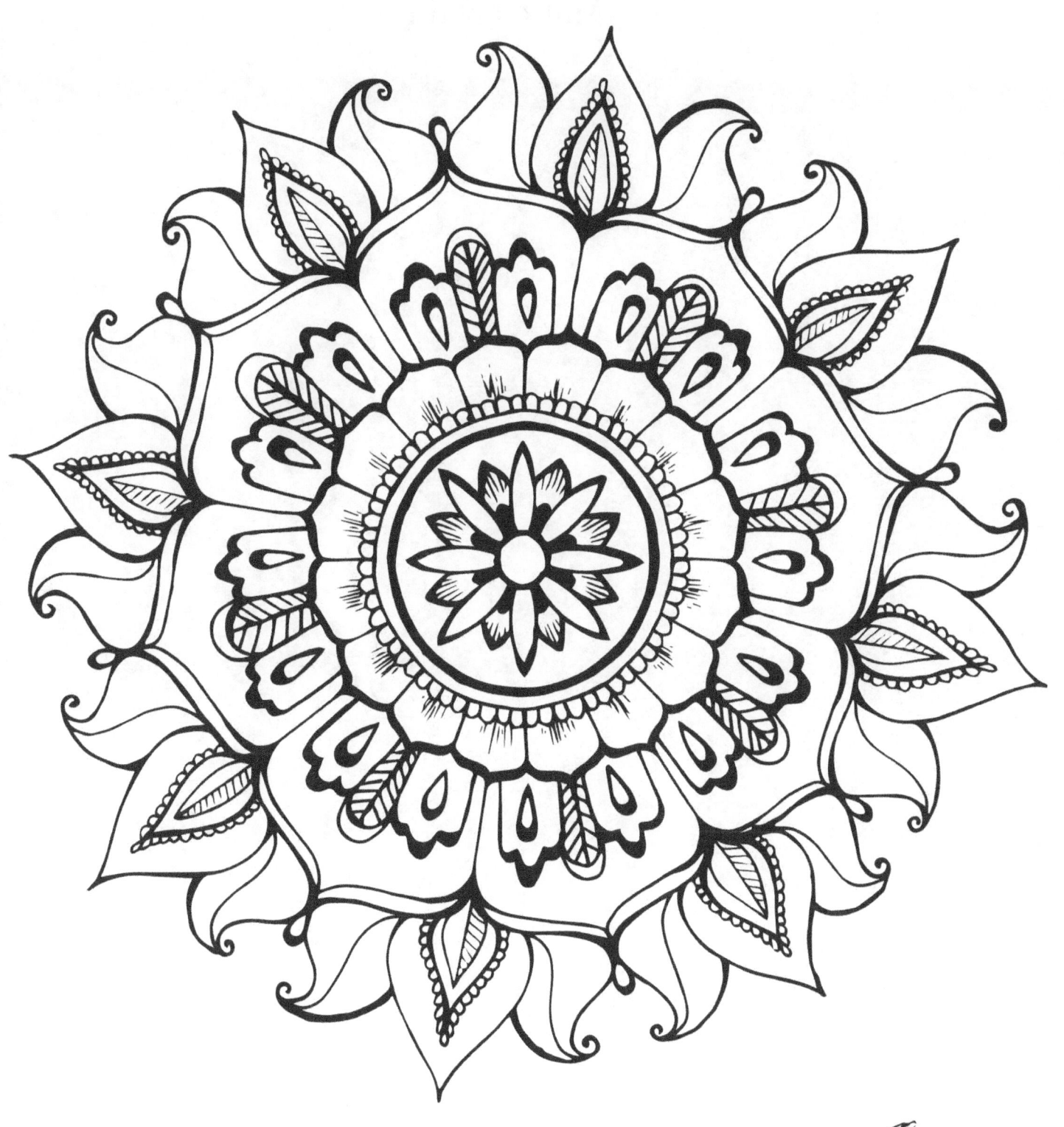

If it's your job to eat a frog, it's best to do it first thing in the morning. And if it's your job to eat two frogs, it's best to eat the biggest one first.
~Mark Twain

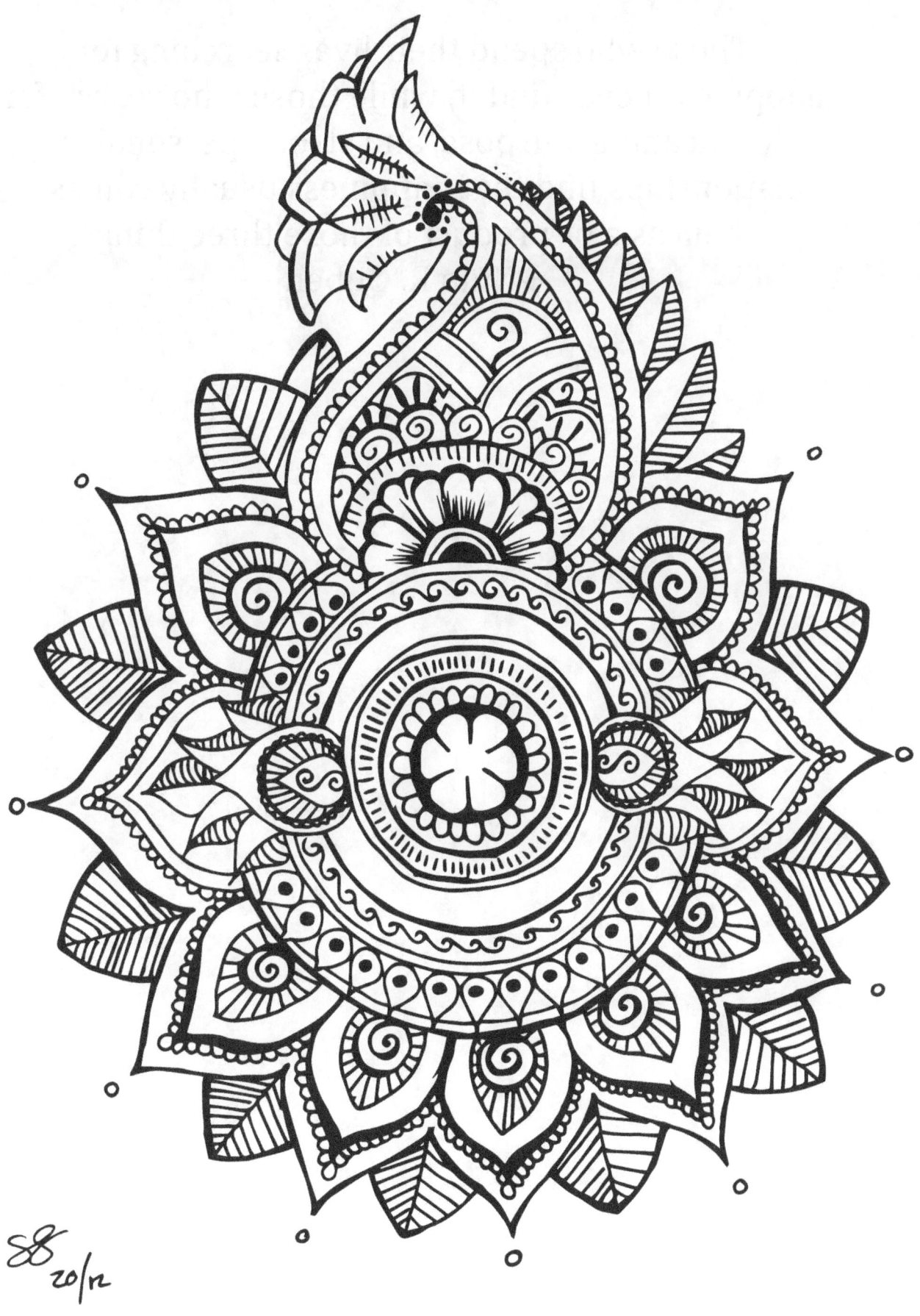

Those who spend their lives searching for happiness never find it, while those who search for meaning, purpose, and strong personal relationships find that happiness usually comes to them as a bi-product of those three things.
~Nido R. Quben

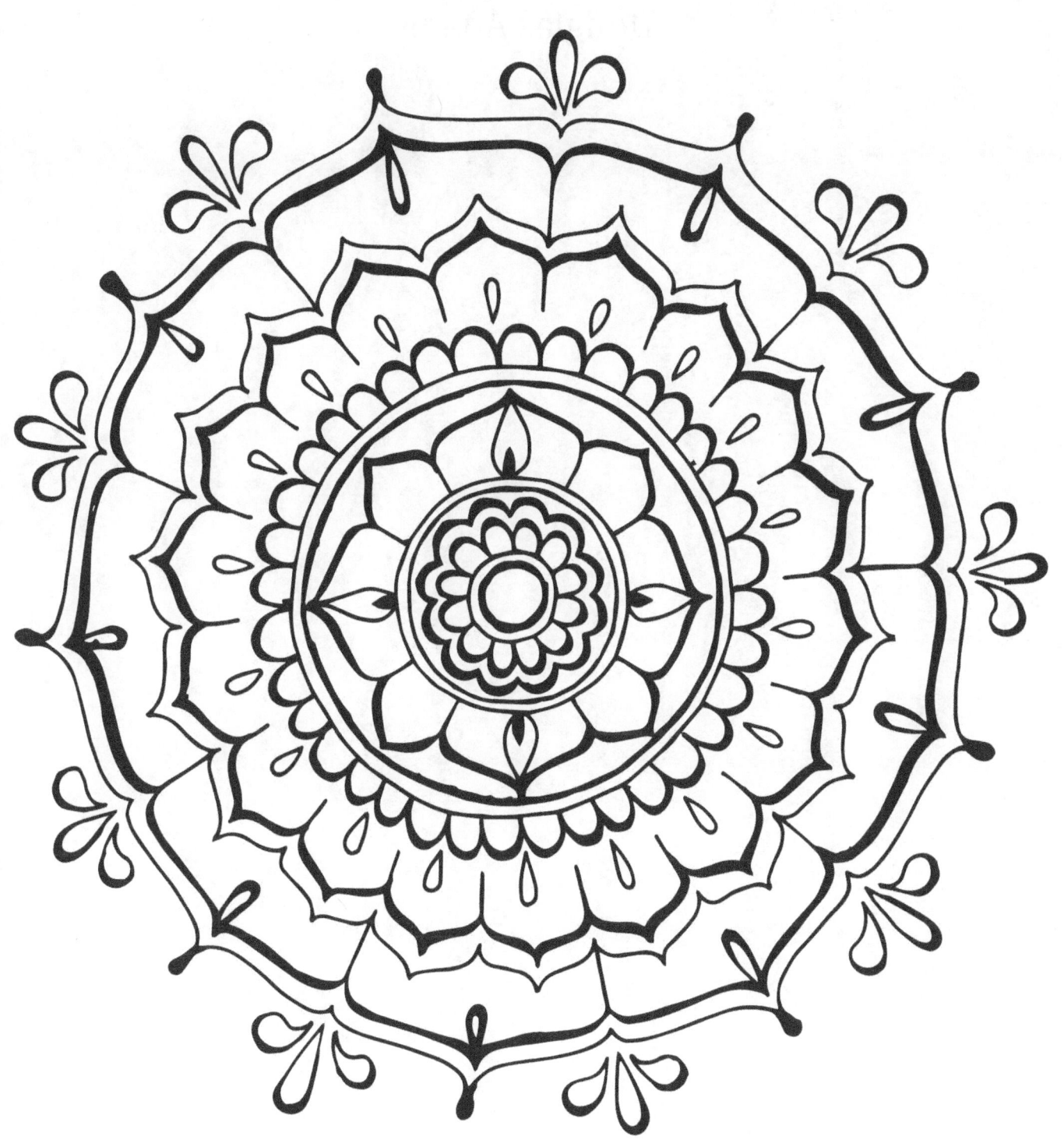

88 1/13

I may not have gone where I intended to go, but I think I have ended up where I needed to be.
~Douglas Adams

Don't ask what the world needs. Ask what makes you come alive, and go do it. Because what the world needs is people who have come alive.
~Howard Thurman

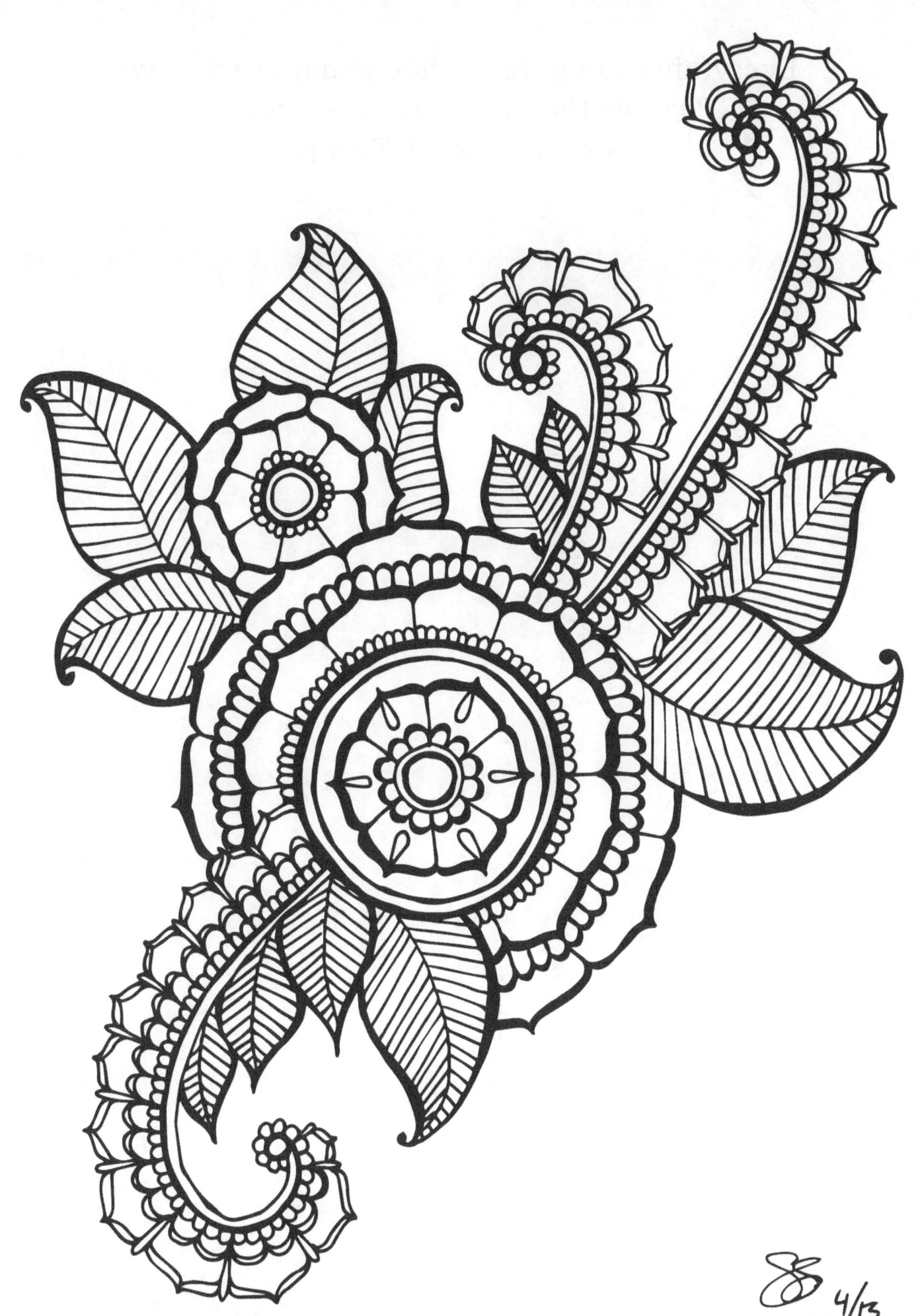

Everything comes to us that belongs to us if we
create the capacity to receive it.
~Rabindranath Tagore

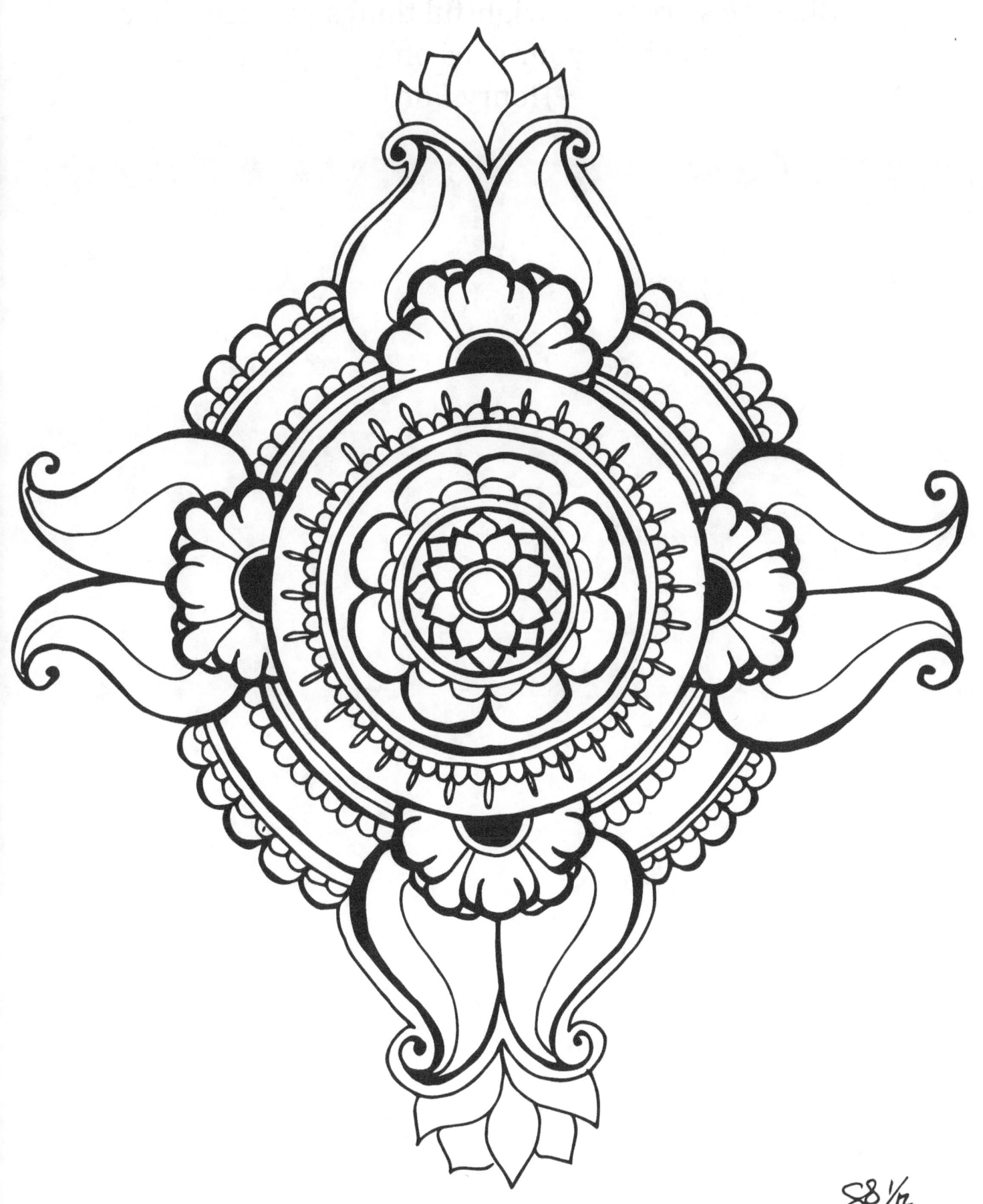

SS 1/12

Obstacles are those frightful things you see when
you take your eyes off your goal.
~Henry Ford

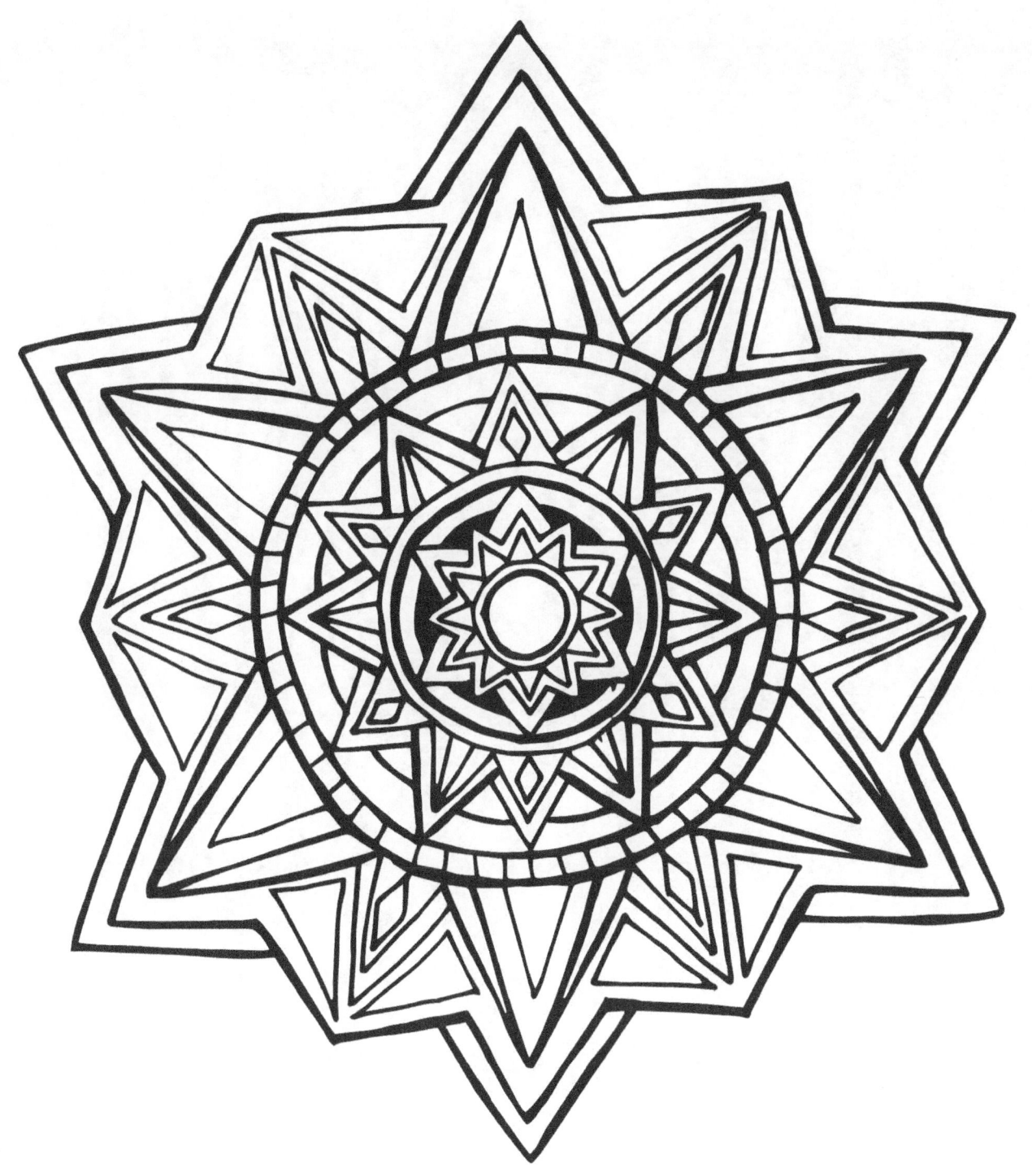

There is no charm equal to tenderness of heart.
~Jane Austen

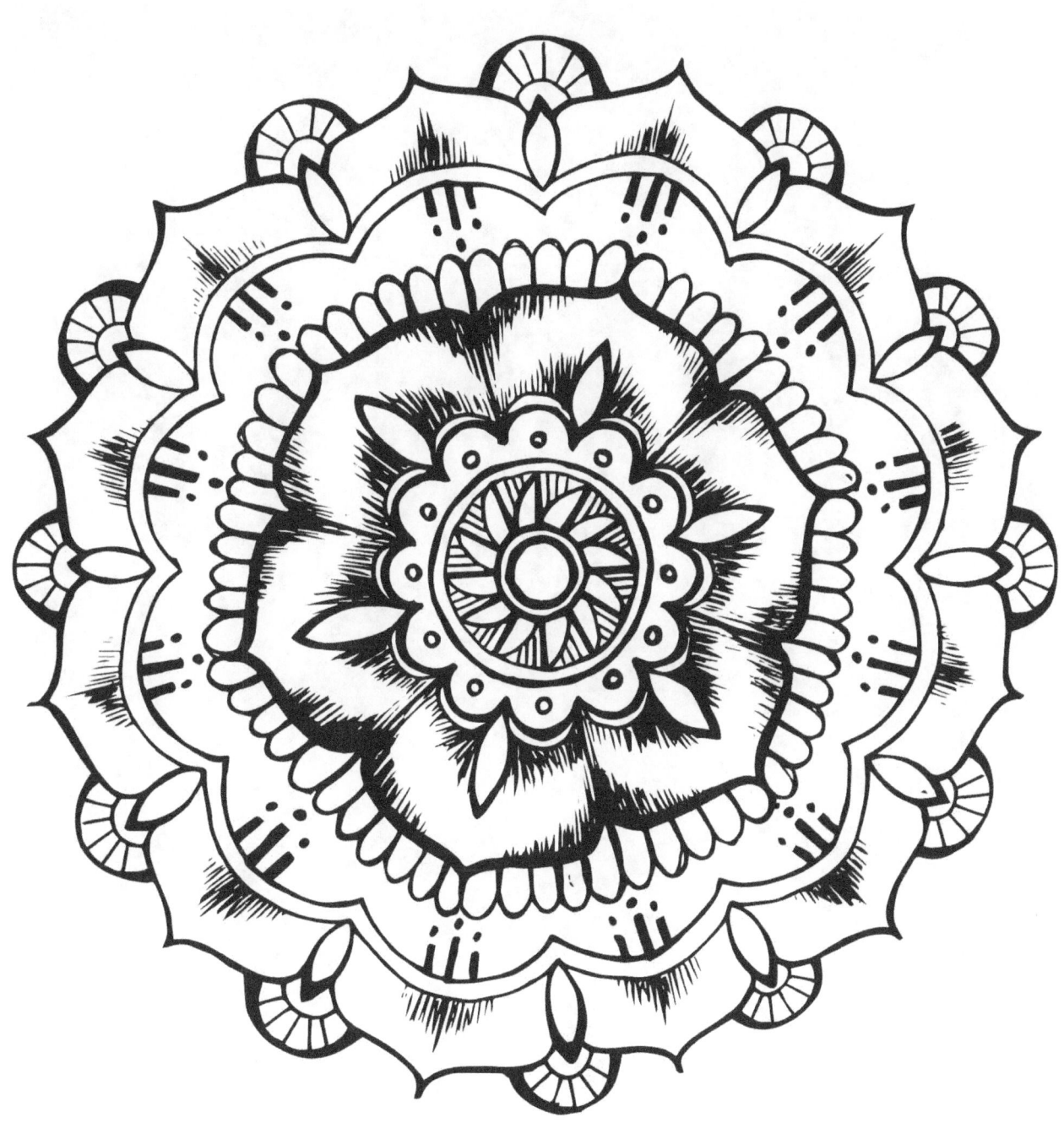

SB 4/15

A tree is known by its fruit; a man by his deeds. A good deed is never lost; he who sows courtesy reaps friendship, and he who plants kindness gathers love.
~Saint Basil

www.ingramcontent.com/pod-product-compliance
Lightning Source LLC
Chambersburg PA
CBHW080624180526
45168CB00007B/3051